For All Those
Saints

O.C. Edwards, Jr.

Dedicated to
A. J. Robinson
who, during the
century of his life,
has better exemplified what
I am writing about
than anyone else
I have ever known.

©1981 Forward Movement Publications, 412 Sycamore Street,
Cincinnati, Ohio 45202. Printed in U.S.A.   ISBN 0-88028-002-6

1.

Two Approaches
To Sanctity

Roman Catholics and Episcopalians alike are often reminded of the saints. Our churches are named after them, we keep their feast days, and in the liturgy we are told that our voices are joined with theirs when we sing: "Holy, holy, holy Lord, God of power and might . . ." In this recognition of holy persons we are joined not only by many other Christian traditions but also by most religions in the history of the world; in the history of religions, though, such persons are generally still alive, while Christians traditionally have thought only of the departed as "saints."

Primitive religions have not distinguished as sharply as contemporary Western ones between what is sacred and secular; their holy persons have included royalty and military heroes as well as religious leaders. There is a sense that all such persons have a special relationship with supernatural power, power that historians of religion refer to by the Solomon Island word, *mana*. These religions do have a regard for the great persons of their past, but that regard is not connected so much with the idea of divine power. Instead these worthies are looked upon as those who gave the group its common identity, those who best exemplify the community's ideals, and those whose conduct is to be imitated. The history of Christian devotion to the saints, however, has involved the recognition of them both as mediators of power and as examples of life.

The cult of the saints in Christianity began when the early church was persecuted by the Roman empire (a persecution that was never as thorough as Hollywood has led many to believe). When a beloved leader was killed in the violence that broke out from time to time, the Christian community dealt with its loss by gathering up the remains of the martyred person, treasuring them, and commemorating the anniversary of the holy death. The first such death after New Testament times, of which we have an extensive record was that of Polycarp, bishop of Smyrna, who witnessed to his faith with his life around 155 A.D. After describing his death, the author of the record of his martyrdom says:

"We later took up his bones, more precious than costly stones and more valuable than gold, and laid them in a suitable place. There the Lord will permit us, so far as possible, to gather together in joy and gladness to celebrate the day of his martyrdom as a birthday, in memory of those athletes who have gone before, and to train and make ready those who are to come hereafter."

This keeping of the death days of martyrs as their "birthdays into heaven" seemed more consistent with the Easter faith of the early church than commemoration of saints on their birthdays on earth. At first each local church developed its own calendar of such commemorations, listing only its local martyrs. In time, churches began to borrow one another's beloved dead, often with an exchange of relics. When the Emperor Constantine was converted to Christianity early in the fourth century and it became safe for Christians to engage in their worship publicly, the observance of the feasts of martyrs became even more enthusiastic and the discovery of relics of martyrs became even more popular. The Latin word for "discovery" was *inventio* which has a charming ambiguity to modern ears since not all the relics thus unearthed can be assumed to be genuine.

In time this devotion became so intense that special shrine churches were built to house relics and elaborate containers called reliquaries were constructed to contain the remains of the martyrs. After the barbarian invasions accompanied the breakdown of Roman civilization, relics were moved from the cemeteries into churches so that they could be better protected. This transfer of the relics was referred to as a "translation" and feasts additional to the death days of the martyrs came to be celebrated on the dates when their relics were transferred and when altars or churches were dedicated to their honor.

After Christianity became legal under Constantine and martyrdom became unlikely in the Roman empire, Christians began to recognize other categories of heroes of the faith. The first group to whom such recognition was extended were "confessors," who had professed their faith under persecution, but whose suffering did not extend to death. Other categories of saints that came to be recognized included the "doctors" (teachers) and theologians who defended the faith against heresy, those who led devotional lives of great self-denial ("ascetics"), and persons who practiced conspicuous charity and service. After the so-called "peace of the church" under the Emperor Constantine when one could no longer become a martyr or confessor, the extreme asceticism of hermits and monks in the desert came to be regarded as the moral equivalent of martyrdom. By the fifth and sixth centuries the cult of the saints came to be expressed in the church's worship with antiphons sung in honor of the saints. Readings about the lives of the saints (Latin: *legendae*) were added to the evening service in the eighth century. There were differences in the devotion paid to the saints in the Greek-speaking East and the Latin-speaking West. The Latin church focused its devotion on relics while the Greeks satisfied their needs for reverence with holy icons of the saints. By the time of Charlemagne the cult of the saints had become so intense that it became necessary to distinguish between the veneration that could appropriately be accorded the saints (Latin: *dulia*) and the worship that could be extended to God alone. (Latin: *latreia*).

As the cult of the saints continued to develop into the Middle Ages, a change began to take place. It was a change of emphasis growing out of elements that had been a part of this veneration almost from the beginning but which now moved into a dominant position. This change was a focus on miracles as the primary proof of sanctity.

Character and the value of holy example remained important. Among saints that were being recognized for their exemplary lives were missionaries; founders of churches, monasteries, and schools; theologians; ascetics; workers of mercy; and Christian statesmen. Indeed, one can note that there were three main channels for Christian service in the medieval period: the royal, the episcopal, and the monastic. Yet the association of the saints with supernatural power had come to predominate over other considerations. The "lives" of the saints came to be a standard form of literary expression and these written lives were more interested in being edifying than in reporting history factually. (It should be remembered that history in our sense is a modern invention.) These "lives" became stereotyped and seemed to compete with one another in seeing which could record the most astounding marvels. It was this tradition of writing about saints, or hagiography, that led some cynic to say that the patron saints of the islands off the coast of Italy all had two things in common: all of them could levitate and none of them could read.

It was some time before the veneration of a particular saint extended beyond her or his own locality. A uniform calendar was slow in coming. In fact there is not yet any absolutely universal list of persons to be commemorated even within Roman Catholicism. By the time of Charlemagne, however, the calendar of the church at Rome did begin to offer some standard for the rest of the church in the, West. The process of recognizing a person as a saint, canonization, was at first a matter of *vox populi,* popular acclamation. In time bishops began to take this authority for themselves, basing their decisions on the biography of the deceased and the miracles that person was alleged to have performed either while still in this life or in response to requests for intercession after death. The transition to canonization by the pope appears to have been gradual. Pope Benedict VI proclaimed Uldaricus to be a saint in 973 A.D., thus being the first bishop of Rome to canonize someone not connected with the church in Rome. By 1234, however, Gregory IX refused to allow saints to be recognized by anyone else. The modern machinery for canonization goes back to Popes Sixtus V (1588), Urban VIII (1642), and Benedict XIV (1734). It took the invention of printing to make it possible for there to be truly universal calendars.

Along with the development of the process for naming saints went the evolution of the concept of sanctity. A saint was defined as a Christian who is known to be in heaven. This definition presupposes the existence of an intermediate state between heaven and hell, purgatory, and presupposes further that the saint is not there. The knowledge that the saint is in heaven could come either through tradition or through canonization. Since the proclamation of papal infallibility in 1870 it has been assumed that the statement of canonization is infallible since it declares that the person in question is a reliable example of Christian living; it is thus a statement about morals, in which Roman Catholics consider the pope to be incapable of error.

Roman Catholics recognize, of course, that the word "saint" can be and has been used in other senses. They know, for instance, that in the New Testament the word could be used to refer to Christians who were still alive and regularly meant any member of the church. Thus many of those called "saints" in the Bible were not saints at all in the modern sense. St. Paul, for instance, addresses the members of his church at Corinth as saints, but as 1 and 2 Corinthians show, many of them were anything but saintly and if they ever got to heaven, they had to change a lot. Few concepts, though, have only one correct meaning. The important thing is to define in what sense you will use a particular word and to be consistent about using it that way.

Whatever may have been the excesses of popular piety in medieval or more modern times, official Roman Catholic theology has never treated saints as sources of supernatural power that were somehow independent of God. It has always been recognized that all grace comes from God whether it is mediated through the intercession of a saint, given directly, or bestowed in some other way. God through Christ takes the initiative in communicating his holiness to his people. The greatest of God's promises is that he has promised his people to make them like himself, holy as he is holy. What that holiness looks like in a human life is perfectly seen, in Jesus Christ. Since the ultimate purpose of grace is to enable that holiness, it can never exist independently of God nor work over against him in building up the kingdom of self.

In English the close connection between the words "holy" and "saint" is not so clear as it is in most languages. The words mean the same thing: a saint is a holy person. Holiness means loving God with your total being and loving

8

your neighbor as you love yourself. Thus *The New Catholic Encyclopedia* is able to say:

> *"When, by divine grace, a person's whole being is, as nearly as possible, governed by the complexus of virtues centered about religion, that state of heroic virtue has been attained that the church recognizes as worthy of the title of saint."*

This is to say that the practice of the theological virtues of faith, hope, and charity is what leads the Christian soul to the beatific vision of God and to the union of charity with him.

The discussion up to this point has been centered on what the saint did while on earth. Thus the appropriate devotional reaction has been praise and imitation. But when attention is transferred to the presence of the saints in heaven, the emphasis is shifted to the powers of intercession that the saints have and use for Christians on earth and in purgatory. (It should be noted here that in the Roman Catholic understanding of this matter grace obtained through the prayers of the saints is not in addition to or separate from the grace of Christ. Rather, their intercession is thought to be one of many channels through which the grace of Christ, the only sort of grace there is, is mediated. His saintly members are coopted in the task of applying the fruits of his redemption to other members more in need of that grace than they.)

Behind this point of view lies the assumption of the "treasury of merit." By this is meant a deduction from the fact that the saints are already in heaven. Their presence there means that they have already received more grace than they needed to escape the punishment of their own sins and what they have left over, therefore, is available to be transferred to someone who does not have enough. (This is not to say, of course, that escaping punishment is the only or even the most important benefit of grace.)

In this Roman Catholic view, it is the need of Christians for powerful intercession that creates the Church's need to know whether a particular departed Christian is a saint; *e.g.,* is in heaven. By knowing who is in heaven, Roman Catholics know whose prayers to invoke. God raises up saints because he wishes their holiness to be recognized. His manner of calling attention to the saints, by this theory, is the miracles that are performed when their prayers are requested. Note that the miracles that count are those that occur after the death of the saint. It is these that show that the particular member of the faithful departed has escaped purgatory and is already in heaven. It is not necessary, therefore, for the saint to have performed any miracles during his lifetime or even to have done anything unusual — whether in the way of spectacular deeds, or in the exercise of particular gifts of mystical experience. The only requirements in this life for becoming a saint are that you love God and your neighbors to the point of heroic virtue, or that you die as a martyr.

Because Christians all belong to the same Body, they all profit from the labor, prayers, and sacrifice of the saints. Thus the distribution of divine grace has been made dependent, at least in part, on the merits and prayers of the saints. Stated that way, this doctrine sounds very Roman. It reflects a truth, however, which has been called "mere Christianity" — that belief which is held in common by all Christians. It is implied by the words of St. Paul in Romans 10:14, 15:

> *"But how are men to call upon him in whom they have not believed? And how are they to believe in him of whom they have not heard? And how are they to hear without a preacher? And how can men preach unless they are sent?"*

We depend on the missionary and evangelistic work of others to become Christians in the first place and we depend on ordained persons for the grace of the sacraments even though they are not themselves the source but only the channels of that grace. And there are many other ways in which we are interdependent upon one another. The main point of uncertainty for Episcopalians about this Roman Catholic doctrine is that it requires that the saints in heaven be aware of the needs of Christians on earth and that they know about our requests for their prayers. There is nothing in the Bible that says that they do — or that they don't. Thus Episcopalians, for whom every necessary belief must be based on the Bible, are free to believe that the saints hear, doubt that they do, or have no opinion on the subject. But they are not free to require any other Episcopalians to agree with them.

There was a time before the Second Vatican Council that Roman Catholic approaches to such subjects as the treasury of merit seemed to many Episcopalians like a quantification of grace, a kind of spiritual bookkeeping. Pious manuals would list the number of days of plenary indulgence; i.e., remission of punishment in purgatory, that one received for reciting certain prayers with and without making the sign of the cross, which, in turn, could be with or without holy water. Pope Paul VI modified the system of indulgences to show that they existed not just to help sinners escape punishment but also to induce fervor for charity. Thus their effect was not just negative in overcoming the results of sin, but the effect was also positive for the inculcation of virtue. In fact he said that no one can receive an indulgence whose heart has not been totally converted from sin! Furthermore, partial indulgences are no longer reckoned in terms of days or years.

This assumption, that miracles that occur when the prayers of departed Christians are invoked is God's way of calling attention to the fact that those Christians are saints who are now in heaven, lies behind the process of canonization. God is, in effect, calling for the recognition of those saints. The Church sets up the machinery by which they can be recognized. One other function served by the process is that it places a limit on the number of the faithful departed who can be regarded as saints. Ten thousand saints had been recognized before 1500 A.D. Since that time, when the canonizing process has been in operation, only 113 additional saints had been canonized by 1903. Another 547 deceased Christians were accorded the lower status of beatification during the same period.

The process leading toward canonization begins when a local Christian who has died begins to acquire what is called a "fame of sanctity." That reputation for holiness is investigated by the local bishop. He sees that the testimony of witnesses is taken in depositions so that there will be enough documentation when the "cause" is further along. If the bishop finds that there is evidence to support the belief that the deceased either practiced heroic virtue or died for the faith, he informs the Vatican that that person's cause can be introduced. Next, anything written by the deceased is checked for its orthodoxy. The Congregation of Rites, which deals with canonizations in the papal bureaucracy, has an elaborate system of checks and balances to see that the burden of proof is constantly forced back on those who advocate the cause. The feeling is that it is better to withhold recognition from many genuine saints than it is to extend it to one departed Christian who is not yet in heaven. One of the reasons for exerting such care is that canonizations are considered to be infallible statements of the pope.

After the check for purity of doctrine, the alleged miracles attributed to the intercessory power of the deceased are investigated. Particular attention is given to the miracles since, if genuine, they are taken as the evidence that God is calling for the recognition of the intercessor as a saint. In the investigation of the miracles the questions asked are, a), did they occur, and b), were they in response to the intercession of that particular person? If everything checks out, the pope then beatifies the deceased. This is to say that the person in question is afterwards referred to as "Blessed." The cult or veneration of someone who has been beatified is not worldwide, but only local or, in the case of a monk or nun, confined to the particular order. If, however, there are further miracles, the church may then proceed to canonize the person as a saint in the full sense of the word. Then veneration becomes universal. A mass and an office are established in his or her honor, churches may take that saint's name, and the saint's relics may be venerated publicly.

The way in which Episcopalians and other members of the worldwide Anglican Communion recognize saints is very different. This is not to say that a number of Anglicans would not agree with the Roman Catholic process and interpretation in every detail. It is only to say that their agreement would be a matter of personal opinion rather than official church teaching. At the time of the English Reformation, no change was made in the calendar for the church year; the seasons that took their shape from major events in the life of Our Lord remained the same and Sundays kept the names they had. The Reformers did reduce the number of fixed holy days drastically, however. This was especially true of saints days. Before the Reformation the Sarum missal which was widely used in England

13

provided for 175 such feasts, but that number was reduced to twenty-four. The only feasts that were retained were those of Our Lord and of the Apostles, Evangelists, and four others: St. Mary Magdalene, St. Michael and All Angels, All Saints, and St. Stephen.

The reason for this radical reduction in the number of feast days was largely practical and moral. Our word *holiday* is a contraction of *holy day* and the trouble was precisely that holy days had degenerated into mere holidays — days off from work. Since the fourteenth century there had been complaints about the number of feasts because these days off were spent more in drinking, gambling and dalliance than in devotion. The spirit of these occasions can be as well suggested to modern minds by the paintings of Pieter Brueghel the Elder as by anything else. The results were bad for employers and employees alike. P. Bissonnade has estimated that at least one-fourth of the possible working days in a year were thus occupied *(Life and Work in Medieval Europe)*.

In addition to the economic and moral objections, there were also some theological objections, especially concerning the dubious historicity of many of the stories. Then, too, there was the question of whether the saints hear our requests for their intercessions. Nothing in the New Testament suggest that they do. The nearest thing to a biblical warrant was thought ot be a passage in the *Apocrypha,* 2 Maccabees 15: 12-16, which has an obviously legendary ring to it. Thus while the collects for most of the Sundays were retained in the English *Book of Common Prayer* (much as they had been in the Latin Sarum missal) the collects for saints days were mostly rewritten, generally to eliminate a reference to invocation. The English Reformers wanted to return to the New Testament usage where "saints" meant all

Christians, living and dead, rather than retain the medieval meaning of departed Christians who are now in heaven as powerful intercessors because of the heroic virtue they practiced on earth. This desire is shown in their elimination of the distinction between All Saints and All Souls. When one looks at the list of feast days retained, it is obvious that they commemorate only New Testament saints and not all of them.

This biblical emphasis in the matter of saints days was consistent with the major theological contention of the English Reformers, the supremacy of Scripture. That position is stated clearly in the sixth of the Thirty-nine Articles of Religion (1571):

> *"Holy scripture containeth all things necessary to salvation, so that whatsoever is not read therein nor may be proved thereby is not to be required of any man, that it should be believed as an Article of Faith, or be thought necessary or requisite to salvation."*

The Articles of Religion also say that the *Apocrypha* is to be read "for example of life and instruction of manners; but yet (the Church) doth not apply (these books) to establish any doctrine." Since 2 Maccabees is in the *Apocrypha,* its account of Judas' vision of the high priest Onias and the prophet Jeremiah in heaven was not thought to be authoritative for belief. The matter was completely nailed down in Article XXII on purgatory:

> *"The Romish doctrine concerning purgatory, pardons, worshipping and adoration, as well of images as of relics, and also invocation of saints, is a fond thing, vainly invented, and grounded upon no warranty of scripture, but rather repugnant to the Word of God."*

In time, Anglican attitudes on the subject were relaxed. While candidates for ordination in the Church of England

15

have had to subscribe to the Articles, the modern form of that subscription has required no more than an admission that Anglican doctrine as stated in the Articles is consistent with biblical teaching. No such subscription has been required of American candidates and the Articles are included in the section of the 1979 Prayer Book labelled "Historical Documents of the Church." Thus the earlier harsh prescriptions are now interpreted to mean no more than that these beliefs do not appear explicitly in the Bible, so no one may be required to believe them as doctrines necessary for salvation. By the same token, they are not explicitly excluded by the Bible either, so Episcopalians may hold them as private views, or as "pious opinions," to use the technical term. The Anglican intention has not been to deny the existence of saints, as Calvin and the radical reformation attempted to do, but rather to put the emphasis on praising them and imitating them rather than on treating them as accesses to power. Probably many Episcopalians believe that the Church Triumphant in heaven prays for the Church Militant on earth. Many also believe in an intermediate state between heaven and hell, but look on it more as a state of purification and preparation than as a place of punishment. All of this, though, is to anticipate later developments, many of which occurred in the nineteenth century.

At the time of the Reformation, Anglicans did not retain the complex distinctions between feasts by which some were classified as greater doubles, some as doubles, and others as either semidoubles or simples. Instead there was a simple division into two categories: Red Letter days and Black Letter days, referring to the color of ink used to list them in the Prayer Book calendar. Red Letter days were the feasts of New Testament saints retained from the Sarum calendar and for each of these twenty-four days there was appointed a collect, epistle, and gospel. These were the only feast days included in the calendar of the 1549 Prayer Book, but the 1552 book had four Black Letter days, those of St. George, Lammas (a word of obscure meaning that does not appear to be a personal name), St. Laurence, and St. Clement. The new calendar that appeared under Queen Elizabeth in 1561 had sixty-four Black Letter days, most of which appeared on the Sarum calendar; in fact, only two did not antedate the Norman Conquest in 1066 A.D.

Basically the Black Letter days represented more of an almanac than a church calendar, since no liturgical observance was called for. These dates were listed for their local and secular associations, for the history they implied and the dates they supplied. It would be impossible to understand Shakespeare without such a calendar handy, for instance. Yet an official book of private devotions (called a "primer"), *Preces Privatae,* published in 1564, added sixty-one more Black Letter days to its calendar and gave evidence that the faithful were at least to recall the example of the saints on their days even if no liturgical observance was expected at church.

The real understanding of what was intended comes out a century later at the Savoy Conference in 1661 when the Anglicans were coming to terms with the Puritans after the Restoration of the monarchy under Charles II. The Puritans objected to the whole calendar, but especially to having the Black Letter days listed in the Prayer Book. The defense that the bishops offered included the following points: a), since the feasts were of human rather than divine origion they did not need scriptural authority; b), the feasts were ancient; c), by observing Hanukkah (John 10:22), Jesus observed a feast instituted by the Church; d), Red Letter days may be holidays, but Black Letter days are "for the preservation of (the saints') memories, and for other important reasons, as for leases, law-dates, etc.;" and e), all the days were not of equal importance. Thus the positive motives for listing saints days were that the example of the saints could be remembered and that many civil events that had been dated by the ecclesiastical calendar in the Middle Ages could also be remembered.

There was no real change in Anglican attitudes toward the saints for 200 years after the Savoy Conference. In the middle of the nineteenth century, however, several factors caused a renewal of interest in them. Several of them are connected with the reappropriation of the Church of England's Catholic heritage associated with the Oxford Movement. Thus a deepened sacramental life made a new openness to the witness of the saints appear quite natural. Then, too, the Romantic Movement saw the Middle Ages as the great age of faith and loved everything medieval from Gothic architecture on down. The new methods of biblical and historical research that were coming into use at the time made the distinction between the New Testament period and the early church seem much less hard and fast than the Reformers had considered it to be. Finally, the Anglican Church was by then no longer just the church in England but was a worldwide communion and a certain amount of variation in liturgy became inevitable. That variation could be extended to the observance or non-observance of saints days. All of these factors played their parts in renewing interest in the saints.

These nineteenth-century trends have continued and resulted in two great periods of liturgical revision in this century, one in the '20s and the other stretching from the '50s to the '70s. Most of the new Prayer Books produced by national branches of the Anglican Communion during the

'20s were conservative, but in the area of the calendar they were more adventurous. The American Prayer Book of 1928 was one of the few that did not include a long list of Black Letter days. It did, however, go so far as to provide one collect, epistle, and gospel that could be used for "A Saint's Day," so at least the principle of a fuller calendar was implied. To spell out the possibilities of that implication, several church publishing houses issued calendars for use by Episcopal churches that drew on a number of sources, including not only the Black Letter days of the Churches of England and Scotland, but also the Roman Catholic missal. There also appeared altar books that assimilated the rite of the American *Book of Common Prayer* to the Roman rite, including the list of saints commemorated. One of these went so far as to include the feast of St. Pius V, the pope who excommunicated Queen Elizabeth and thus finally made official the separation of the Church of England from the Church of Rome.

The first official effort to provide a fuller calendar for the Episcopal Church that met with any success was the publication of *Prayer Book Studies IX,* one of the pieces of research conducted in preparation for the liturgical revision that resulted in the 1979 Prayer Book. There had been a draft calendar drawn up in connection with the revision of 1928, but that was largely ignored at the time. In commenting on the basis of its selection of heroes of the faith to be commemorated, *Study IX* points out that, "The modern Anglican, living in an age and environment of realistic and scientific criticism, is less inclined to be impressed by the miraculous and legendary elements of the lives of the saints that moved earlier generations to enthusiastic devotion." Its authors also admitted that they were less committed to the norm of biblical personages than the editors of the 1549

19

Prayer Book. Admitting that there were "traditionalists, sentimentalists, (and) romanticists" who were motivated by other considerations, the authors said that they were nevertheless convinced that the majority of Episcopal clergy and laity could be, ". . . attracted to a conscious devotion to the saints only when the particular individual proposed for commemoration is shown on good historical evidence to have exhibited both distinguished service in the cause of Christ and exemplary personal holiness."

It is to be noticed that the emphasis here, as in all Anglican thinking about saints, is upon their exemplary lives rather than upon the power that they mediate. The result of our devotion to the saints is intended to be that we will imitate them rather than that they will intercede for us. As noted above, it is probable that many Anglicans believe that the faithful departed pray for the church on earth; but at the same time, most are agnostic about the existence of purgatory or the ability of the saints to be aware of our requests for their intercessions. Thus the only canonizing process in which we are likely to have much interest is simply the inclusion of noteworthy Christians from the past in our calendars. This makes the Anglican approach very different from the Roman Catholic emphasis upon canonization as an infallible judgment about the presence of the sainted person now in heaven and about the intercessory power of that person as demonstrated through miracles. Episcopalians still have as their fundamental theological conviction the assumption that there is nothing central to the Christian faith that is not clearly taught or implied in the Bible. The only change in that conviction is that it is now modified by and filtered through the historical/critical method of biblical interpretation.

2.
Anglicans In The Calendar Of Saints

The difference between Roman Catholic and Episcopal attitudes toward saints has been explored by seeing the difference between the processes by which someone who has practiced heroic virtue is included in the calendar of one communion or the other.

Another way of getting at what is distinctive about the Anglican point of view would be to look at the persons who are included in our calendar to see what attributes they have in common, thus isolating the qualities that we admire and which we consider to be holy. We will be considering only Anglicans. By Anglicans we mean communicants of the Church of England since the Reformation and members of other national branches of the Anglican Communion. Not included in this group, therefore, are a large number of British saints who lived before the Reformation, even though there are many of those in the calendar. These include Celtic saints from before the time when close ties were established between England and the see of Rome under Gregory the Great as well as non-Britains who were active in the evangelization of Britain and British missionaries who were active in the conversion of Northern Europe.

Before moving on to those who are included it is worth noting some of the persons regarded as saints who do not appear in the 1979 calendar. Not surprisingly, Joan of Arc is not there. It is hard for the English church to get very enthusiastic about the divine guidance of a person whose primary accomplishments were French military victories

21

over the English. Yet there are limits to the Anglophile bias of the list: Blessed Charles, King and Martyr, does not appear on it. Even though it can be said that his life would have been spared if he had been willing to give up having bishops in the church and that his personal life was quite moral, the facts remain that; a) he was not a very good king; and, b), his feast was originally instituted more for reasons of patriotism (one could almost say party politics) than religion.

St. George, the patron of England, is omitted because almost nothing is known about him and few contemporary Episcopalians believe in dragons. Both he and St. Christopher were excluded from the Roman calendar for lack of historical record and neither appears in ours for the same reasons. Another principle of the formation of our calendar was that the only post-Reformation saints to be included would be Anglicans. (This is not to suggest that only Anglicans have been holy, but is to recognize the sad fact of our division and the impossibility of including everyone worthy of commemoration in a manageable list of observances.) The great leader of the Oxford Movement, John Henry Newman, is excluded because he became a Roman Catholic and was even made a cardinal. On the other hand, John and Charles Wesley do appear, even though they founded the Methodist movement, because they never did break formally with the Church of England.

It is not to be expected that even all Episcopalians would be equally enthusiastic about each person selected for the calendar. Part of the genius (and the curse) of the Anglican Communion is its capacity for compromise. Because of the tensions that have always existed between those who wish to emphasize the Catholic and those who wish to emphasize the Protestant heritage of Anglicanism, one does not have to be too cynical to speculate that some of the people in the 1979 calendar represent trade-offs between Anglo-Catholics and Evangelicals or Liberals. At any rate, that "hermeneutic of suspicion" offers an easy way to begin an analysis of the list.

First the Catholics. *William Laud* (feast: January 10) was Archbishop of Canterbury under Charles I and, like his king, was executed for treason under Oliver Cromwell. He was a great supporter of the divine right of kings and he was harsh in his treatment of Roman Catholics and Puritans, especially the latter, though not so harsh with them as they proved with him and others. He was a staunch High Churchman and his policies were the basis of the settlement after the restoration of the monarchy; thus he had much to do with the shape that Anglicanism has taken ever since. The great tragedy in his life has been well stated by the English church historian, J. R. H. Moorman:

> *"He had the misfortune to think he was born to set the world right. In no circumstance could he ever suffer a fool gladly. No allowance was made for carelessness or weakness; no attempt was made to meet people half-way; no plea of ignorance or misunderstanding was ever listened to . . ." (A History of the Church in England).*

Certainly *John Keble* (March 29) and *Edward Bouverie Pusey* (September 18) deserve to be listed among the Anglo-Catholics. With John Henry Newman they made up the central leadership of the Oxford Movement, the Catholic revival of the Church of England in the nineteenth century. (This movement is also known as "Tractarianism" because of the group's publication of their views in a series of pamphlets called "Tracts for the Times." Another name given it at the time was "Puseyism," a term that was used so widely that it was even spotted in a Greek newspaper). This movement to reawaken the sacramental life of the English church is usually said to have begun with Keble's sermon preached before the judges of Assize in Oxford on July 14, 1833. Called "National Apostasy," the sermon lashed out against a Parliamentary proposal to reduce the number of bishops in Ireland. The issue was not a practical consideration of how many Anglican bishops were needed there, but was whether the government has the right to tell the church the number of bishops it needs. Keble, who was Professor of Poetry at Oxford for ten years, is well known for his book of religious verse, *The Christian Year,* from which numbers 155 and 166 in *The Hymnal 1940* were taken. Most of his ministry — over thirty years — was spent as priest in a country village. Pusey, on the other hand, spent most of his active life as Regius Professor of Hebrew at Oxford and Canon of Christ Church cathedral there. He had studied in Germany and was the only man at Oxford in his time who knew German. He considered the new biblical criticism that was developing there to be a threat to Christian orthodoxy, a view held by Anglo-Catholics before Bishop Charles Gore. Pusey did much to restore appreciation of Christ's Real Presence in the Eucharist, the practice of private confession, and monks and nuns to the Church of England.

James DeKoven (March 22) is associated with the American appropriation of the Oxford Movement. He taught Church History at Nashotah House, a seminary founded under Tractarian influence, but he became far too "advanced" for the Nashotah faculty of that time and so he moved to Racine, Wisconsin, where he became Warden of Racine College. He was twice elected to the episcopate but could not be consecrated because some dioceses withheld their consents over his churchmanship. His old colleagues on the faculty at Nashotah House campaigned against him in the Diocese of Wisconsin, saying that he would make the Episcopal cathedral in Milwaukee indistinguishable from the Roman Catholic one — something that eventually occurred without his help. The depth of his devotion, though, impressed many who disagreed with him sharply, and he was exceptionally influential in General Convention. The Community of St. Mary now keeps the campus of Racine College as a retreat house known as The DeKoven Foundation.

Names included in the calendar to please Evangelicals could begin with *William Tyndale* (October 6). Tyndale was a Reformer and Bible translater who spent most of his adult life in exile because of persecution by Henry VIII and the church. It is ironic that perhaps eighty percent of his translation survived in the King James version that became authorized for the Church of England and was indeed the basis of most early English translations. His reforming zeal went further in Lutheran and Zwinglian directions than most of the English church did. Eventually he was martyred under the Holy Roman Emperor, Charles V. His famous goal was to make it possible for even a plow boy to know the Bible better than the Bishop of London.

Ten days after the feast of Tyndale is that of three of his contemporaries who did much to bring about the Reformation for which he prepared the way: *Hugh Latimer, Nicholas Ridley,* and *Thomas Cranmer.* Because he believed in royal supremacy in the church and conscientiously consented to help Henry VIII get an annulment of his marriage to Catherine of Aragon, Cranmer was made Archbishop of Canterbury and thus implemented most of the English Reformation. Probably his greatest contribution was his editorship of *The Book of Common Prayer* on which his exalted prose style made such an impact. Latimer was

Bishop of Worcester and Ridley of London; they had supported Cranmer and the Reformation cause under Edward VI and thus came in for unfavorable attention at the time of Queen Mary's return of the English church to papal obedience. Latimer and Ridley were made to debate with Roman theologians, then were condemned for heresy, confined to the Tower of London, and burned at the stake. Latimer's last words are said to have been: "Be of good comfort, Master Ridley, and play the man; we shall this day light such a candle by God's grace in England as (I trust) shall never be put out."

Other Evangelicals must certainly include the founders of the Methodist movement, *John* and *Charles Wesley* (March 3), who have been mentioned above. Also to be mentioned is *Charles Simeon* (November 12), a late contemporary of the Wesleys who worked completely within the framework of the Church of England. He was converted when he had to receive Holy Communion at King's College, Cambridge, and was thrown into despair by his sense of a need for preparation. When he graduated he became the priest of Holy Trinity Church in Cambridge. He was ridiculed for his Evangelical views at first, he had the church locked against him, and he was often mobbed and assaulted in the streets when he walked from his college to the church. In time, his deep piety and powerful preaching won over his opposition and he became one of the most influential persons in not only Cambridge, but the entire Anglican Communion. The historian Macauley said that he was more influential than the Archbishop of Canterbury. He was one of the founders of the Church Missionary Society and the British and Foreign Bible Society.

If there were trade-offs between Catholics and Liberals for the calendar, *Phillips Brooks* (January 23) probably needs to be listed among the latter, although he was too conservative and orthodox to be limited to any party. Most of his life was spent in Boston as Rector of Trinity Church and Bishop of Massachusetts, but he was always first and foremost a preacher — probably the best Anglican preacher of his century. It is too bad that he is now remembered chiefly as the author of "O Little Town of Bethlehem."

Another of the principles of selection that seems to be involved in the list of Anglican saints in the American calendar of 1979 appears to be that of historical significance. Quite a number of those commemorated were involved in key transitions in church history. For instance, the largest group on the list are missionaries. While the tribute paid to them is in part a matter of commitment to the conversion of the non-Christian world, there is also a recognition that these persons were the founders of our church in their part of the world. Most of these represent what Kenneth Scott Latourette, the historian of the missionary movement, called "the great century of expansion" — the nineteenth century. Not surprisingly, a high percentage of these missionary saints were also martyrs, having witnessed with their lives to the faith that had taken them to every corner of the world.

America has sent so many missionaries to other parts of the world that it is a little shocking to be reminded that there was a time when missionaries needed to be sent here. One of the most important Anglican missionaries sent to the American colonies was *Thomas Bray* (February 15). Although the word "episcopal" means "having bishops," the Church of England, which was to become known as the Episcopal Church in America after the Revolution, existed from 1607 to 1784 without bishops. During that time the church in the American colonies was theoretically under the Bishop of London, but he seldom did anything to exercise his oversight. This meant that any American who wished to be ordained had to go to England and that no one could be confirmed during all that period. It also meant that there was neither anyone to defend or discipline the clergy nor anyone to spearhead the missionary work of the church among the Native American people or among the whites engaged in westward migration. The main reason why bishops were not consecrated for America was that those in England at the time were so involved in the life of the privileged classes that no one could yet imagine the democratized episcopate that would develop in this country.

Bray was appointed by the Bishop of London to become his "Commissary" through whom he would exercise his oversight of the churches in America. While Bray came to America only once and then stayed only two and a half months, he went home to labor tirelessly for his co-religionists on this side of the Atlantic. His interests ranged from the training of clergy to their morals and fidelity to their calling, from the religious education of children to the foundation of theological libraries, from missionary activity among slaves and Indians to concern for those confined to prison in a barbarous age. Among his accomplishments were the founding of the Society for the Propagation of the Gospel (S.P.G.), which sent many well-trained and devoted priests to the American colonies, and the Society for Promoting Christian Knowledge (S.P.C.K.), to publish and distribute Christian literature. Both of these institutions still exist and continue in the good work for which Bray founded them.

A contemporary of Bray, *Henry Martyn* (October 19), was interested in carrying the Gospel to another part of the world. While serving as curate to the great Evangelical, Charles Simeon, Martyn decided to go to India in 1805 as a chaplain with the East India Company in Calcutta. His desire to reach beyond the English colony there and evangelize the native people did not please his employers who were apprehensive of any religious disturbance of the country. Since he was a gifted linguist, Martyn was able to convey the Good News of Christ by translating parts of the Bible and the *Book of Common Prayer* into Hindi, Persian, and Arabic. His only Indian convert, Abdul Masih, was the first Indian ever to be ordained by an English bishop. Before his premature death at the age of thirty-one, Martyn had also planted the church in Persia (Iran).

George Selwyn (April 11) went even further east, becoming Bishop of New Zealand in 1841. He was so successful in establishing relations with the native people there, the Maoris, that during a ten-year period of war he continued to be trusted by both sides. Much to his regret, he was brought home to England to be made Bishop of Lichfield. A friend of Selwyn at Eton, *John Coleridge Patteson* (September 20) grew up to follow him to the Pacific as a missionary in Polynesia and Melanesia. Since he was there under Selwyn's jurisdiction, the Bishop of New Zealand had a see that covered half of the Pacific Ocean. Having gone out in 1855, Patteson was made bishop in 1861. Going from island to island, he set up churches and schools, doing much to improve the condition of native peoples. Tragically and ironically, he was put to death in 1871 by some islanders who thought that his ship was another English slaving ship. His death roused the English to enough indignation to put an end to this inhuman traffic which had been outlawed in England and the West Indies fifty years earlier. The Christian descendants of Patteson's converts during World War II saved the lives of many American servicemen.

There were other martyrs among missionaries and

converts in Africa during the nineteenth century. Uganda gives us both *James Hannington And His Companions* (October 29) and *Martyrs Of Uganda* (June 3). Hannington began missionary work in Africa in 1882 and was consecrated as Bishop of Equatorial Africa two years later. The next year he and his companions were speared to death as they approached Uganda because the local ruler, Prince Mwanga, a Muslim, thought that Christians were trying to enslave his people. Hannington's dying words were: "Go tell Mwanga I have purchased the road to Uganda with my blood." The persecution of Christians lasted three years. In 1964 Pope Paul VI set aside a feast for the converts who perished in that persecution, mentioning that both Roman Catholics and Anglicans were involved. These Ugandan martyrs are probably our only shared post-Reformation saints, since each church counts among its other martyrs saints who were slain by the other church. Uganda is the most predominantly Christian country in Africa today as a result of this missionary activity and witness in blood. Indeed, as we shall see in the next chapter persecution is not yet ended there. Archbishop Janani Luwum was put to death by Idi Amin almost exactly a century after Bishop Patteson died.

Another African missionary martyr is *Bernard Mizeki* (June 18), who was born in Portuguese East Africa and escaped to Capetown where he was converted by an Anglican missionary. In 1891, at the age of thirty, he volunteered as a catechist in a pioneer missionary venture into Mashonaland. When there was an uprising there against Europeans and their friends, Mizeki was warned that he had been especially marked out for death, but he refused to leave his converts. The Church in Central Africa regards him as its primary native martyr.

In the Far East, *Channing Moore Williams* (December 2)

became Bishop of Japan just at the time that the Shogunate was deposed and the Emperor was restored to power. During that period Christianity benefited from the attraction all things western held for the samurai, the warrior class occupying a social position between the nobility and the common people. Taking advantage of the situation, Bishop Williams began to open schools — first a seminary and then what became St. Paul's University, Tokyo. While Anglicans constituted a relatively small Christian group in Japan, the Bishop anticipated future growth and need by organizing the church there as an independent Anglican province called *Nippon Sei Ko Kai* (usually translated "The Holy Catholic Church of Japan"). Soon he had founded six dioceses. By this time a nationalist reaction had set in, but Anglican progress was not checked seriously. Williams had originally been appointed Bishop of Japan and China, but he gave up his responsibility in China to concentrate on Japan. After his retirement he stayed on in Japan to help his successor. He continued to open new mission stations almost until his eightieth birthday. Then he returned to the States to die in Richmond two years later in 1910.

Ten years after Bishop Williams gave up his jurisdiction over China a new bishop was appointed there who was one of the most remarkable men in the history of the Episcopal Church. Born of Jewish parents in Russian Lithuania, *Samuel Isaac Joseph Schereschewsky* (October 15) came to America by way of Germany where he was interested in Christianity by English missionaries to the Jews. He came to America and went first to a Presbyterian seminary and then to The General Theological Seminary. In 1859 he went as a missionary to China, where he began translating the Bible. He was made bishop in 1877 but had to resign his diocese six years later because of a stroke. During his active episcopate

31

he had accomplished many good things such as founding St. John's University in Shanghai. He was one of the most eminent scholars of oriental languages in his day. He was so paralyzed that the only way he could write was to type with the middle finger of his right hand, but in that condition he translated the entire Bible into Easy Wenli, creating a manuscript of 2,200 pages. His comment on this experience shows how much he deserves to be included in our calendar of saints: "I have sat in this chair for over twenty years. It seemed very hard at first. But God knew best. He kept me for the work for which I am best fitted."

Another missionary to the Far East was *Charles Henry Brent* (March 27). A Canadian by birth, he had tested his vocation as a monk with the Society of St. John the Evangelist in Boston and then became the rector of a parish in the slums of Boston where he served with imagination and effectiveness for ten years. He was elected Bishop of the Philippines when the United States acquired the islands at the end of the Spanish-American War. The idea was not that the Episcopal Church would compete with the Roman Catholics there, but rather that it would minister to those Rome had not reached: the English-speaking part of the population, and the Igorots, Moros, and Chinese. As virtually chaplain to the administration, Brent worked to see that the natives were not exploited and that they moved toward self-rule. He also began a crusade against the opium trade.

His philosophy of missionary work was that one should begin by learning what was going on and how to fit in. He did not feel bound to the Prayer Book since he was working with the entire community. Then, too, it was better to begin with the moral conscience than with efforts to convert. Missionaries should be committed to their work and not regard it as the stepping stone to something better. Finally, he thought that a personal, pastoral ministry was more important than setting up an organization.

During World War I he was Chaplain to the Supreme Headquarters of the American forces. After that he came back to the States to become Bishop of Western New York. Perhaps his most important work came out of his insight into the way that the divisions of Christendom interfered with Christian witness and missionary work overseas. Thus he inspired the Faith and Order Movement that preceded the organization of the World Council of Churches.

The last (and latest) saints from the Pacific area are the *Martyrs Of New Guinea* (September 2) who were executed by the Japanese during World War II. These include eight missionaries and two Papuans. As noted above, many Papuans constantly risked their lives to care for the wounded. Normally saints are not recognized until at least fifty years after their deaths, but the death of these Christians was so obviously for their faith that it seemed natural to the church in that part of the world to begin to commemorate their sacrifice quite early.

This discussion of missionary saints in the calendar began with one who came to America. It can conclude with two who served on our western frontier. Because of its close connections with England, the Anglican church in America was in poor repute and badly depleted after the Revolution. Its weakened condition left it with little energy to participate in the early stages of the migration to the westward frontier. It was not until 1835 that General Convention recognized that the whole church is a missionary society and tried to elect two bishops to spearhead the Episcopal Church's participation in the country's western expansion. The man elected for the Southwest would not serve, but *Jackson*

Kemper (May 24) was more than willing to take on the responsibility for planting the church in Indiana, Wisconsin, Minnesota, Iowa, Missouri, Kansas, and Nebraska.

Among the many institutions he founded is one that still serves the church today, Nashotah House, the seminary in Wisconsin near which he made his home and settled down finally to be bishop of only one state. He had begun Nashotah House by recruiting three young graduates of The General Seminary to come out west and found a religious order — the first Anglican experiment in monasticism since the Reformation — and use that as a base for mission among both the settlers and the Indians. They were also to found a school that would train frontiersmen for ministry on the frontier.

The leader of these three young clergy was *James Lloyd Breck* (April 2). After several years the monastic ideal faded; one of the three returned east, another married Kemper's daughter, and only Breck remained. He moved on to take his ideals with him, but a solidly based seminary loyal to the traditions of the Oxford Movement was left behind. After some work with the Chippewa at Gull Lake, Minnesota, he moved to Faribault and founded a remarkable set of church institutions in what was just a frontier village at the time. Among these was the first cathedral of any American diocese (still standing and beautiful) and Seabury Divinity School, which merged in 1933 with Western Theological Seminary in Evanston, Illinois to become Seabury-Western Theological Seminary. One gets the impression that pioneer saints were not always easy to live with. At any rate, Breck, who had married in the meantime, went to California to found yet another seminary at Benicia, which has not survived, although parishes he formed out there are still very much a part of the church.

After missionaries, the next most prominent group of saints in the Episcopal calendar of 1979 represent an almost uniquely Anglican phenomenon. This group includes those who have written classical books on the spiritual life, which means that they were ascetics and teachers. (It also means that they were gifted writers and in fact some of them are better known in the history of English literature than in church history.) Before listing them, it is worthwhile to note that the '79 calendar includes one pre-Reformation figure who has not been canonized by the Roman Catholics: *Thomas à Kempis* (July 24), the author of *The Imitation of Christ*.

The first of the Anglican spiritual writers to be mentioned is *Lancelot Andrewes* (September 26), who, with the following five to be considered, was a representative of one of the great flowerings of the English church during the time of King Charles I, from which they are known as "The Caroline Divines." Andrewes was bishop of several sees at one time or another, the last of which was Winchester; he was one of the translators of the King James version of the Bible. Although he was a great preacher and a favorite court prelate in three reigns, he had little interest in politics. Probably his most famous work and that most often reprinted is his collection of private prayers in Latin and Greek collected from many sources and published along with his own comments under the title *Preces Privatae*.

The most famous poet in this list is certainly *John Donne* (March 31). The leader of the metaphysical school of poetry, Donne had come from a devout Roman Catholic family. During his youth, he led a profligate life that is reflected in some rather bawdy poetry that he wrote at the time. Trained as a lawyer, he had hoped for a political career that had every promise of brilliance until he secretly married the

35

daughter of his patron and employer, the Lord Keeper of the Great Seal. This marriage was thought to be such a breach of trust that Donne and his rapidly growing family were cut off from all support until finally, after much searching of conscience, Donne, who had become an Anglican, acted upon the urging of James I and was ordained. His stunningly beautiful religious poetry seems to have been written largely during the period of his disfavor. After ordination his genius was poured into his preaching. When he became Dean of St. Paul's, the cathedral of the Diocese of London, he attracted huge crowds.

Almost as famous a poet was *George Herbert* (February 27). Most of his life was spent at Cambridge where he was a Fellow of Trinity College and the university's Public Orator. At the age of thirty-six, however, he married and thus had to give up his fellowship. He then took the small country parish of Fuggleston-with-Bemerton near Salisbury and remained there until his death four years later. His ideal of what such a ministry should be was written in *A Priest to the Temple, or The Country Parson, His Character, and Rule of Life.* He also wrote a book of religious poems called *The Temple* from which the text of two hymns, numbers 290 and 476 in *The Hymnal 1940,* were taken. So effective was he in his ministry that when he went each day to his church for Morning Prayer at ten o'clock and Evening Prayer at four, most of his parishioners were present. The famous writer on fishing, Isaak Walton, also wrote on the Anglican Caroline Divines. In his *Lives* he wrote that many people working in the fields "let their plough rest when Mr. Herbert's saints-bell rung to prayers, that they might also offer their devotions to God with him."

The person to whom Herbert gave *The Temple* was his friend *Nicholas Ferrar* (December 1). Ferrar retired from prosperous business ventures at the age of thirty-four, took deacon's orders, and withdrew to form a religious community at Little-Gidding with his mother, his brother and sister and their families, and many servants. Together they led a simple life and practiced great charity to the poor in the neighborhood, to whom they gave their best rather than their castoffs. All performed manual labor and they started a school. The community rule included four times for prayer during the day (Morning and Evening Prayer and two periods of intercession) and they shared a night vigil in which the entire Psalter was recited. The community kept going for ten years after Ferrar's death in 1637, but they had so scandalized the Puritans with what was considered to be their "popery" that Little Gidding was sacked and burned after Oliver Cromwell came to power. Their community inspired much that has come since, including the last of T. S. Eliot's *Four Quartets,* "Little Gidding." Of the pilgrim to that place he says: "You are here to kneel/Where prayer has been valid."

Jeremy Taylor (August 13) was one of the Caroline Divines who lived through the time of Cromwell to see the Restoration of the monarchy and Anglicanism under Charles II. A brilliant scholar, he served as chaplain both to Archbishop Willain Laud (see above) and to King Charles I. During the Commonwealth he went to Wales as private chaplain to a nobleman. It was during that period that he wrote his most famous book, *Holy Living and Holy Dying.* After the Restoration he became bishop in the Irish see of Down and Connor.

Thomas Ken (March 21) is best remembered for his hymns, although it is doubtful that many of the millions of Christians who love to sing the Doxology he wrote have any idea who wrote it. During his life he might have been most famous for taking public stands against royal personages with whom he was closely related: he refused to allow Nell Gwyn, the mistress of Charles II, to be quartered in his house while he was a Royal Chaplain, for which Charles admired him, had him appointed as Bishop of Bath and Wells, and made his deathbed confession to him. When James II became a Roman Catholic, Ken opposed the change of laws that would have given more civil liberties to Roman Catholics and Puritans, for which he was sent to the Tower of London. When the case was finally settled in court, though, it was one of the main events in the downfall of James. When William and Mary were called to the throne to succeed James, Ken felt that the oath of allegiance that he had taken to James prevented him from being able to swear allegiance to them! Thus he became a part of the Non-Juring schism from the Church of England, although he was never at ease in that position. In fact, he was reconciled to the church when Queen Anne came to the throne. His dying words show the spirit of the times:

"I die in the Holy Catholic and Apostolic Faith, professed by the whole Church, before the disunion of East and West: more particularly I die in the communion of the Church of England, as it stands distinguished from all Papal and Puritan innovations."

William Law (April 9) was a promising young scholar when George I came to the throne. Law felt that he could not take the oath of allegiance to him because he thought the Stuart heirs of James II were still the rightful heirs to the English crown. Like Ken, though later than he, Law was a Non-Juror. For that reason he could not be given a parish in the Church of England and lived most of his life as the private chaplain of the wealthy who did not object to his views. Yet he was much involved in the theological questions of his day, especially the Deism that was so popular then. Law is best known as a spiritual writer. Although greatly influenced by the mystic, Jacob Boehme, his own most famous book, *A Serious Call to a Devout and Holy Life,* was not far removed from the experience of the ordinary Christian. If the measure of a person's accomplishment is the influence she or he had on others, Law was one of the greatest. Samuel Johnson said that Law was the first major religious influence on his life. Law was also well spoken of by his former pupil, Edward Gibbon, the freethinking historian of *The Decline and Fall of the Roman Empire.* And he made a considerable contribution to the development of the thought of John and Charles Wesley.

The last person to be included in the list of spiritual writers lived well after the others and died only a little over a century ago. *John Mason Neale* (August 7) could have been listed among the partisan favorites of Catholic-minded Episcopalians because he belonged to the later, ritualistic or "millinery" phase of the Oxford Movement — a phase quite different from the more theological earlier period. Neale was, for instance, the first English priest for several centuries to wear a chasuble for the celebration of the Eucharist. His ritualistic practice led to his being forbidden to exercise his priesthood for sixteen years. He was one of the founders of the Cambridge Camden Society, later called the Ecclesiological Society, that did so much to encourage the revival of Gothic architecture and medieval vestments and ceremonial in the Church of England. While his interests may sound precious, Anglican worship as it is known today would hardly be recognizable if it were not for the influence of Neale and like-minded persons. Certainly our hymnody would be greatly improverished; almost forty hymns written or translated from the Greek or Latin by him are included in

The Hymnal 1940. He was also the founder of the Sisterhood of St. Margaret, which did much to educate and relieve the suffering of women and girls — in spite of its meeting great resistance when it was founded.

While our calendar includes many missionaries and spiritual writers, not surprisingly it includes few saints who are known chiefly as theologians. Our communion has not been bound together around theological formulas as some denominations. Commitment to the community of the church, its liturgy, and its history has been the cement that has held us together. Thus it has been said that Anglicanism is more of an orthopraxy (a system of correct practice) than it is an orthodoxy (a system of correct belief).

Perhaps the greatest theologian among us has been *Richard Hooker* (November 3). Hooker was born and came to maturity during the reign of Queen Elizabeth. At Oxford he was a pupil and protege of one of the great defenders of Anglicanism, John Jewel. After being ordained and married, he left his teaching job at Oxford to hold a series of country parishes. When he was called to become Master of the Temple in London, he discovered that his assistant, the Reader, Walter Travers, was teaching the Calvinist view that the Bible reveals the correct form of church government and worship and that nothing is to be allowed that is not explicitly called for in Sciputre. In response, Hooker wrote the classic statement on Anglican doctrine, *The Laws of Ecclesiastical Polity,* in which he argued that not everything in the church is or should be of direct divine institution. Rather, God, the source of reason, gave human beings intelligence to arrange many things for themselves. In religious matters, therefore, we are to be guided by reason and tradition as well as by revelation.

While there was too little trust in reason in Hooker's time, there may have been too much of it during the so-called Enlightenment. The English phase of the movement saw the development of a strain of theological thought called Deism. The Deists believed that the power of human reason was so great that supernatural revelation was unnecessary; all one needed to know about God was revealed in the orderly processes of nature, which showed that the world came into being through the design of an infinite Mind. Being so devoted to the order of nature, the Deists were shocked at the idea of an interruption of that order by miraculous intervention ascribed to God. The self-confidence of England in the eighteenth century was so great that it was assumed that Diest convictions were obvious to every thinking person.

One to whom they were not so obvious was *Joseph Butler* (June 16), later to become Bishop of Durham, who, while still priest of a small country parish, wrote *The Analogy of Religion, Natural and Revealed, to the Constitution and Course of Nature*. This book, which is still published, answered all of the arguments of the Deists without mentioning those who held them. Its basic thesis is that the order of nature which is so important to the Deists is not widely visible, but is known in only a few areas that have been investigated. One has to argue from the part to the whole that there is harmony throughout the universe. The analogy between religion and nature is not discovered by self-sufficient reason (natural revelation) alone, but is fully made known only by supernatural revelation. All opponents of the Deists were not accepted by Butler as allies, however. To the greatest of them, John Wesley, Butler said: "Sir, the pretending to extraordinary revelations and gifts of the Holy Ghost is a horrid thing, a very horrid thing." In a 1739 sermon supporting a mission to slaves in the West Indies

Butler became one of the first church leaders we know to have declared that black people are fully human and have souls.

Frederick Denison Maurice (April 1) cannot be fitted into the partisan strife between Evangelicals and Catholics that so dominated church life in mid-nineteenth century England. He was instead caught up in concern over the impact of the industrial revolution on the lives of the urban poor. Slum conditions, overcrowding, poor sanitation, the labor of women and children were the issues that occupied his attention. This was a time of exploitation and a period of Irish immigration to London. There was a wide-spread fear that the French revolution might be repeated in England. Maurice was in favor of the Chartist movement for human rights and he was the founder of the (non-Marxist) Christian Socialist Movement. Seeing education as necessary for the laboring classes, he founded the Working Man's College. He was dismissed as professor of theology at the University of London because his teaching on whether the damned are punished eternally was thought to be unorthodox. He was the founder of Queen's College for women and later taught at Cambridge. In his theological reflection on society and in his concern for Christian social action he became the forerunner and inspiration of much that occupies twentieth-century theology. Perhaps his most famous work is *The Kingdom of Christ*.

The only American Episcopal theologian to achieve a world reputation was *William Porcher DuBose* (August 18). Descended from a French Hugenot family in South Carolina, he studied at the Citadel, served both as a staff officer and as a chaplain in the Confederate army, and became a deacon near the end of the war. He served parishes in his native state until he became a professor at the University of the South in 1871. He served as Dean of the School of Theology at Sewanee from 1894 to 1908. He taught for twenty years before he began to publish his thought. He was a close student of the New Testament and familiar with classical theological literature, but he was hardly in touch with the theological writings of his time. His contribution to theology is usually said to be that he added to it the dimension of psychology, and that he did so before Freud. (What is meant, though, is not psychology in the sense of a social science. Rather, he saw the implications of personal life for theology and vice versa.) His theology might be said to be "existential."

The last category of persons included in the 1979 calendar is that of those whose significance lies in their influence on the life of the church. Only one in this category is not an American: *William Wilberforce* (July 30) a wealthy layman and member of Parliament who was one of the great early Evangelicals in England. He used his position in Parliament to labor for social reform and is credited with doing more than anyone else to bring English participation in the slave trade to an end. He was also a great supporter of public education and foreign missions.

One of the feasts commemorates an event rather than a person: *The Consecration Of Samuel Seabury* (November 14). It has been noted that the church in the American colonies got by without a bishop from the founding of Jamestown in 1607 to 1784 when Seabury was consecrated Bishop of Connecticut by Scottish bishops.

The first person in this country to try to revitalize the Anglican church after the Revolution was *William White* (July 17). In a pamphlet called "The Case of the Episcopal Churches in the United States Considered," he called for a national church organization based on a federal constitution.

Knowing that the English might not be willing to consecrate American bishops, White suggested that the church might get along without them if it had to. The Connecticut clergy, however, were shocked at this, thinking that an Episcopal church without Bishops was either a contradiction in terms or a new thing under the sun. Many of them, after all, were converts from Congregationalism and could not bear to give up much of what had attracted them to Anglicanism. Seabury, who was something of a stuffed shirt and had been a chaplain in the British army during the Revolution, was devoted to apostolic order and the sacraments and willing to endure whatever it took to find and persuade some Anglican bishops, somewhere, to consecrate him. His action forced other American dioceses to act and England decided at last to cooperate: on February 4, 1787 in Lambeth Chapel, William White was consecrated Bishop of Pennsylvania and Samuel Provoost Bishop of New York. White, who had been chaplain to the Continental Congress, lived to a ripe old age and founded many good causes. He was the first Presiding Bishop of the Episcopal Church.

A contemporary of Seabury and White and, indeed, one of White's clergy, was *Absalom Jones* (February 13), the first black priest of our church. Born a slave in Delaware, Jones early showed a deep desire for an education and a strong attraction to religion. When he was moved to Philadelphia he found opportunity to study at night school and also managed to earn enough to buy freedom for his wife and himself. He became a lay minister to the black parishioners of a church of another communion, but his success in evangelism caused the church officers to segregate blacks into an upstairs gallery in the church. The black members withdrew from the white church and founded their own with Jones and his close friend Richard Allen as their ministers. The two went different ways, with Jones becoming rector of St. Thomas, Philadelphia, a parish still in existence, and Allen founding the African Methodist Episcopal Church.

Another man ordained by Bishop White was *John Henry Hobart* (September 12), who became Bishop of New York and did much to move the Episcopal Church beyond a mere survival mentality after the American Revolution. He actively involved the church in missionary expansion westward. There is an old joke that the Baptist preachers walked west with the members of their congregations, the Methodist circuit riders followed soon after on their horses, and the Episcopal priests took the first train. Hobart was one of those responsible for seeing that they got on the train. He also was one of the founders of General, the first of our seminaries, and started what is now Hobart and William Smith Colleges. He was an ardent advocate of the sort of high church theology that preceded the Oxford Movement.

If most scholars of church history had to name the greatest leaders the Episcopal Church has produced, they would undoubtedly name *William Augustus Muhlenberg* (April 8). Of him the Episcopal historian, James Thayer Addison, has written:

> *"Until the last years of his long life he was always starting something new. Since the general tendency of the Episcopal Church in his day and long thereafter was never to start anything new, we need not be surprised that Muhlenberg was soon a notable and often a lonely figure (The Episcopal Church in the United States)."*

He founded Flushing Institute, the first of many boarding schools under Episcopal auspices. He started a church college, St. Paul's, at Church Point, Long Island. Many of his innovations appeared in a parish he founded at what is

45

now the corner of Sixth Avenue and Twentieth Street in Manhattan, the Church of the Holy Communion. His sister's legacy from her husband enabled the parish to operate without a pew rent. Here Morning and Evening Prayer were said daily, a weekly Eucharist was celebrated, a boy choir sang, and many other things were done that must have seemed startling at the time. While Muhlenberg knew of the Oxford Movement and actually visited Newman and Pusey in Oxford, he was not a Tractarian but rather someone with a natural sense of the "beauty of holiness" and the holiness of beauty. But he was not a mere aesthete; he was a pioneer of Christian social concern and organized many programs to help the poor. He was also a pioneer ecumenist whose views were publicized in *The Evangelical Catholic,* a journal he founded. St. Luke's hospital in New York is another of his foundations. His "Memorial" to General Convention in 1853 was an effort in liturgical reform and ecumenical initiative for which the church was not yet ready. He was always a "sturdy dreamer" who could envision great improvements in the life of the church and then labor capably to translate his dreams into reality. Influenced by such great men as Jackson Kemper and William White, he influenced others, including James Lloyd Breck.

Perhaps the man closest to Muhlenberg in stature was *William Reed Huntington* (July 27), who, among other extraordinary accomplishments, made General Convention a powerful instrument for church reform. He is best known as the inspiration of the Chicago-Lambeth Quadrilateral, that statement which defines the Holy Scriptures, the Creed, the sacraments of Baptism and Eucharist, and the Apostolic Ministry of bishops, priests, and deacons as the basis upon which the Anglican Communion will consider union with other Christian bodies (1979 Prayer Book, pp. 876-78). Huntington also was the guiding spirit behind the revival of the order of deaconesses (now, women deacons) and behind the Prayer Book revision of 1892.

This concludes the list of Anglicans commemorated in the calendar of the 1979 Prayer Book. We have noted that it includes members of both the Catholic and Evangelical parties, missionaries, martyrs, and founders of national branches of the church, spiritual writers in great abundance, only a few theologians, and persons who have shaped the life of the church. By studying the list one can discover the forms of heroic virtue that Episcopalians most admire: among them, missionary zeal or a pioneering spirit; personal devotion; strong churchmanship (either high or low); intellectual and literary gifts, political effectiveness (even in defeat); skill in organization and building of enduring institutions.

There are also notable omissions. Obviously, all the saints in the American calendar are men. One could try to blame the society of their time, yet we commemorate women from the New Testament period and the early church, as well as the middle ages. And Roman Catholics include a number of Post-Reformation women in their calendar. Maleness remains, evidently, a prerequisite for Episcopal sainthood. In addition, while there may be too many founders of religious orders included in the Roman calendar, there probably are not enough in ours. Other deficiencies could probably be noted. But, by and large, these saints would seem, *a priori,* to incarnate the virtues that are the Anglican ideal of sanctity.

3.
Candidates For
Future Calendars

In an effort to arrive at an understanding of what makes a saint, a comparison has been made of the ways that Roman Catholics and Anglicans include members of the faithful departed in their calendars. A study has also been made of members of the Church of England and its sister churches in the Anglican Communion who have been commemorated in the new American calendar. So far, our analysis has focussed on categories of persons recognized rather than on the qualities of personal holiness and heroic virtue that contributed to their choice. Does that suggest that what one does is more important for canonization that what one is?

To a large extent this is true. There is no doubt that there are countless persons who have lived quiet lives of self-giving love for God and neighbor who may not have been noticed for that even by those who knew them best. That recognition gives us All Saints' Day and was dramatized beautifully by C. S. Lewis in his account of an imaginary bus ride from hell to heaven in *The Great Divorce*. The narrator tells of seeing a procession in heaven:

"*All down one long aisle of the forest the under-sides of the leafy branches had begun to tremble with dancing light. . . . Some kind of procession was approaching us, and the light came from the persons who composed it.*

"*First came bright Spirits, not the Spirits of men, who danced and scattered flowers — soundlessly falling, lightly drifting flowers, though by the standards of the ghost-world each petal would have weighed a hundred-*

weight and their fall would have been like the crash of boulders. Then, on the left and right, at each side of the forest avenue, came youthful shapes, boys upon one hand, and girls upon the other. If I could remember their singing and write down the notes, no man who read the score would ever grow old. Between them went musicians: and after these a lady in whose honour all this was being done."

The narrator thought the lady to be the Blessed Virgin Mary. He was told, however, that she was a very ordinary persons in the world's eyes, one who had lived in an ordinary London suburb. Yet she had showered a non-possessive love on all who came within her orbit — children, animals, and even a manipulative husband, whom she understood completely, although she never stopped caring for and being tender toward him.

I once heard Massey Shepherd say that the best sort of Christian education is knowing a saint. I know that is true because I was vicar once of a small mission that had such a person as its Senior Warden. (He is A. J. Robinson to whom this book is dedicated.) Rob was in his eighties then and I was a young priest, just beginning my graduate study so I could teach in a seminary. He was very concerned that I was trying to do too much. He wanted to come by and put out our garbage every week and help with other chores. I had to be careful to mow the lawn of the vicarage and the adjacent church before it really needed it, to keep Rob from coming over to do it with a hand mower in the hot Texas sun. Almost every day he and his wife would come by in the late afternoon — surely the hardest time of day for the parents of small children — and take our two-year-old son and sometimes his infant brother off to see the train go by.

He did as much for many others as he did for us. The small

children at St. Paul's were convinced that he was St. Paul —it was his church, wasn't it? He taught church school and swept the floor. He went fishing with other vestrymen and would lean against a tree around a campfire in the evening, a can of beer in his hand, and recite English poetry from memory as long as anyone wanted to hear it. He could do the same in Latin. He was Tail Twister in the Lion's Club and, being a retired teacher, tutored teenagers who were having difficulty. I never presumed to ask him about his prayer life, but I know that grace had worked in him a more trans-figuring love for all people than I have ever been aware of in anyone else.

When we were on sabbatical in California recently, we were able to stop and visit with him, a few months before his hundredth birthday. He had taken to wearing tennis shoes to make him a little steadier on his feet, but otherwise he was much as we remembered him. He could recall more of my activity when I was his parish priest than I could. We found out that the little autobiographical volume he had written a couple of years before had been completed before his son and daughter-in-law, with whom he lived, had discovered that he was even thinking about it. He was full of plans for travel: to go back for the anniversary of the Texas high school coaches association, of which he was a charter member, and to attend the convention of Lions International in Chicago.

No one occupies a more privileged position in my personal calendar than Rob. To see him was to know what Christianity is all about. But his was always inevitably a local commemoration. To be a saint in the calendar of a wider community, one must have lived a more public life and have been better known. That is why categories of persons are easier to abstract from calendars than qualities of life.

In some ways this would seem the ideal time for the recognition of persons who have practiced heroic virtue in a public arena since mass communications make it so easy for anyone who does anything in the least extraordinary to come to the attention of many more people than ever before. Television allows millions of people to see and hear anyone who attracts public attention. One result of the technology of electronic media is that we now have "celebrities" — persons who are, in the phrase of Daniel Boorstin, "famous for being famous." Anyone in the country can become extraordinarily familiar with celebrities. Television can expose such a depth of intimate detail that we come to know more about their private lives than we often know about those of our nextdoor neighbors.

We lose perspective, in all this knowledge, of the intrinsic value of the person. Indeed, as George W. S. Trow, Jr. has pointed out:

"Television has a scale. It has other properties, but what television has to a dominant degree is a certain scale and the power to enforce it. . . . The trivial is raised up to power. The powerful is lowered toward the trivial." ("Reflections Within the Context of No Context," New Yorker 11/17/80).

The difficulty in dealing with religious personages on tv is in knowing whether the trivial has been raised to power or the powerful has been reduced to triviality. Again, as Boorstin has said, since news is not generated in a constant flow, it must be created to fill the uniform slots of space or time that are provided for it. The result is media-created events or, as Boorstin calls them, "pseudo-events," that are celebrity-centered.

It is inevitable that many of the potential saints for future calendars who will be discussed in this chapter will have received some attention from the media and will have been the objects of mass adulation. Even though a degree of public recognition is necessary for canonization, the tv media scale that gives importance to the trivial and trivializes the important makes it an unreliable indicator in itself of persons to be considered.

In the discussion of Anglican saints in the 1979 Prayer Book it was noted that some on the list could be considered trade-offs between Anglo-Catholics and Evangelicals. That does not imply that the persons in either category did not deserve to be included. One of the great achievements of Anglicanism is its recognition that glory is not one-sided. The love of God and neighbor is a "many-splendored thing." Thus whatever political considerations went into its formation, the calendar had at least the virtue of showing that, since God's glory has an infinite number of facets, it may be reflected from innumerable angles. Yet the list of candidates for future calendars has no trade-offs in the sense of trying to please everyone. Each person listed below is thought to have some legitimate claim for recognition as a saint. While all of them are not my own favorite nominees, they represent an effort to guess at what a list compiled by concensus might look like. It is by no means confined to Anglicans, but it does have a preponderance of them simply because the limitations of my experience leave me more familiar with the outstanding persons of my own tradition than with those of other traditions.

This list, too, has its missionaries and martyrs, although they are as likely to be indigenous leaders of young churches as they are to be Europeans or Americans who have gone to take the gospel to the Third World. As a matter of fact,

Christianity today is often a more flourishing enterprise in former colonies than it is in the countries that originally colonized and evangelized them.

There is no more obvious candidate with whom to begin than *Mother Teresa,* the Yugoslav nun whose work among the "poorest of the poor" in Calcutta has spread around the world. Certainly she has captured the popular imagination, being featured on English television and the subject of Malcom Muggeridge's book, *Something Beautiful for God,* appearing on the cover of *Time* magazine and receiving a Nobel prize. For some time her Congregation of Missionaries of Charity was the only Roman Catholic religious order that was growing rather than declining. Having gone to India as a Sister of Loretto, she received her "call within a call" to leave the covent and serve the poor in 1946. After three months of medical training, she went into the Calcutta slums to begin a school for children in the open air. Her order was officially founded in 1950 with twelve members, but in less than twenty-five years it numbered 700 sisters and 100 brothers who lived in fifty houses around the world. She added to the three traditional vows of poverty, chastity, and obedience the fourth vow of "whole-hearted free service to the poorest of the poor — to Christ in his most distressing disguise." In 1952 she founded the Nirmal Hriday (Pure Heart) Home for Dying Destitutes in which beggars are taken in from the streets and cared for lovingly while they await a death with dignity. By 1957 she had begun to work with lepers. Her work expanded in the early '60s to Ceylon, Tanzania, Australia, Venezuela, and Italy. Since then it has spread out even farther.

The man who captured the public imagination in the '40s and '50s the way that Mother Teresa has in the '70s and '80s was *Albert Schweitzer.* The son of a Swiss pastor,

Schweitzer astounded Europe with his outstanding achievements in three widely different fields: music, theology, and medicine. He became the substitute organist in his father's church at the age of nine and grew up to become one of the best known interpreters of Bach both on the organ and in a biography he wrote at the age of thirty, in 1905. He had been busy doing other things, too. In 1899 he received his Ph.D. for a study of the religious philosophy of Immanuel Kant and became curate of St. Nicholas' church in Strasbourg. Within four years he was acting principal of his theological college and teaching New Testament at the university. His inaugural writing for his teaching post, *The Quest of the Historical Jesus,* revolutionized the interpretation of Jesus in German scholarship. He continued his work in the parish, working especially among the homeless and prisoners. In 1904 he read an article on the needs of mission work in the Congo and felt the call to become a medical missionary. By 1913 he had received his M.D. (writing a thesis on the inappropriateness of efforts to psychoanalyze Jesus) and had played concerts to raise money for his mission. He had married in 1912 and his wife trained as a nurse to go with him to Africa as his only companion.

In Lambarene, French Equatorial Africa, he built a hospital that was like a native village to which members of a patient's family came to cook and to nurse. During the seven-year interruption of his work, caused by World War II, he continued to think and write. It was at this time that he coined the phrase that best sums up his philosophy, "reverence for life." He wrote on the philosophy of civilization, the place of Christianity among world religions, St. Paul's mysticism, and the writings of Goethe. After he rebuilt his hospital, help came from all over the world and with it came enormous recognition, including a Nobel prize and designation as "the greatest man alive" by a popular news magazine.

The growth of Christianity in Africa has been phenomenal. When Schweitzer went to Africa there were only slightly more than a million Christians south of the Sahara. By 1950 there were more than twenty million. That number doubled in the next decade and more than doubled in the decade following that. It is projected that over half of the Christians in the world will be African by 1990. Uganda has been one of the countries where evangelistic activity has been most successful; today more than half the population is Christian (split nearly equally between Roman Catholics and Anglicans). Idi Amin, who seized power in the beginning of 1971, adopted policies favoring his own Muslim religion which made up only about 15% of the population. Estimates vary considerably, but before he himself was driven from power, he was thought to have put to death somewhere between thirty thousand and three hundred thousand Ugandans. He came to believe that Christians in general and Anglican bishops in particular were resisting his efforts to establish a dictatorship and leading the opposition against him. Early in February, 1977, troops came in the night to search the home of Archbishop *Janani Luwum* for arms he was believed to be importing for an insurrection.

Luwum, had grown up in an Acholi village and helped his father herd cattle, sheep, and goats. He had been sent to school to receive teacher training in hopes that he would become a chief. Though he did begin a teaching career, he underwent a dramatic conversion experience during the East African Revival that turned his previously nominal Christianity into the motivating power of his life. Those through whom he had been converted arranged for his training first as a lay reader and then for ordination. His education was eventually to include a year's study in England. By 1974 his leadership was so pervasive that he was the natural choice of the Ugandan church to become its new archbishop.

During the time that preceded his final capture by government forces, he continued to preach: "We must love the president. We must pray for him. He is a child of God." At the same time, Anglican and Roman Catholic leaders were also calling on Amin to restore due process and to stop the murder of his own people. On February 16, 1977 Amin called a meeting of government officials, members of the armed forces, ambassadors, and religious leaders. That meeting turned into a mock trial of the bishops in which they were accused of importing arms. After the crowd, including the other bishops, was dismissed, Archbishop Luwum was told that he was wanted by the president. He was never seen alive again. Although a story was released that he had been killed in a car wreck, it was known that he had been shot to death, possibly by Amin himself. Before he left to obey the summons of the president Luwum's last words to his fellow bishops were: "I can see the hand of the Lord in this."

Another recent martyr was Archbishop *Oscar Arnulfo Romero* of El Salvador, who was killed by an assassin on March 24, 1980, while he was saying mass in the chapel of the Hospital of Divine Providence in San Salvador. Originally something of a conservative, Archbishop Romero had grown increasingly outspoken in his opposition to the regime of Dictator Carlos Humberto Romero, who had used what amounted to gestapo tactics to impose his will on the country. Seven priests were among those killed by government forces and many other church leaders had been beaten or tortured. When the dictator was overthrown in the autumn of 1979, Romero supported the new junta under

Jose Napoleon Duarte, but it soon became apparent that repression would continue. After that Romero began to speak out against the new government. The identity of the murderer and, therefore, the reason behind the murder has never been established. In his homily just before his death, the archbishop said: "I am prepared to offer my blood for the redemption and resurrection of El Salvador. If God accepts the sacrifice, I hope it will be a seed of liberty and a sign of hope." Such a statement of the doctrine of vicarious suffering seems appropriate for the religious leader of a country whose Spanish name means *The Savior*.

With missionaries and martyrs, recent years have also produced a number of candidates for inclusion in future calendars who are writers. Most of these have not been religious writers in the technical sense, although at least *Baron Von Huegel* and *Evelyn Underhill* qualify in that way. Friedrich von Huegel, the son of an Austrian diplomat and a Scottish convert to Roman Catholicism, was born in Austria and had a cosmopolitan upbringing and education before he finally settled in England. Well read in all the sciences, as well as philosophy, history, and biblical criticism, he was closely associated with the Roman Catholic Modernists, although he escaped being included in their condemnation by Pius X in 1907. It is chiefly as a writer on the spiritual life that he is remembered, and he was highly regarded as a spiritual counsellor. One of the many persons he influenced was Evelyn Underhill, the daughter of a London lawyer, who was converted to Christianity at the age of thirty-two and quickly became an authority on religious experience in both its theoretical and practical aspects. She wrote a number of books on mysticism and a comprehensive study called *Worship* in addition to editing works of medieval mystics and ancient eucharistic prayers.

Some of the greatest apologists for Anglicanism during the twentieth century, however, have also been among the best known writers in the language. These include two of the most influential poets of the century, English scholars who published fantasy, science fiction and children's stories, a novelist of the supernatural, and one of the all time great detective story writers. *T. S. Eliot,* born in St. Louis, educated at Harvard, the Sorbonne, and Oxford, emigrant to England, teacher, bank clerk, and editor, received the Nobel Prize in Literature in 1948. His early work, which was as influential as it was complex, expressed the anguish and barrenness of modern life. The theologian, Paul Tillich, might have said that he was asking existential questions that were a demand for revelation. At any rate, he espoused Anglo-Catholicism in 1927 and his later works are informed by a powerful religious vision, as may be seen in *Four Quartets;* dramas such as *The Rock, Murder in the Cathedral,* and *The Cocktail Party;* and in essays like *The Idea of a Christian Society.*

It has been said that after W. B. Yeats and Eliot died, the greatest living poet in the English language was *W. H. Auden.* Auden reversed Eliot's path, being an Englishman who settled in America. It is appalling to think that two of the greatest literary artists of our age were forced to support themselves by other work, Eliot by editing and Auden by teaching. Auden came from a clerical English family and said that if he had not become a poet, he probably would have been an Anglican bishop. He even attributed much of his poetic skill to the precision of enunciation he was taught as a choirboy. Like that of Eliot, his early work showed more concern for social diagnosis than remedy, and he rejected most of the middleclass values with which he had been brought up, including Christianity. He was strongly attracted to the Republican side during the Spanish Civil War and was close to becoming a Marxist. It was the Second World War that convinced him that more than poetry was needed in the face of fascism. He began to read Kirkegaard and Reinhold Niebuhr and was re-converted to Christianity and Anglo-Catholicism in the early '40s. His Christmas oratorio, *For the Time Being,* and his *Age of Anxiety* represent the early stages of his Christian period.

From the early '30s through World War II a group of friends gathered twice a week in Oxford, once at a local pub and the other time in the rooms of one of the group, to talk about matters of mutual interest and to read to one another from books they were in the process of writing. They were bound together by a classic taste in literature that eschewed most things modern, by commitment to the Christian faith, and a love of the literature of myth and fantasy. They called themselves "the Inklings." For our purposes the most important members of the group were *C. S. Lewis, J. R. R. Tolkien,* and *Charles Williams.*

Lewis, who has written distinguished literary criticism on the literature of courtly love, the seventeenth century, and Milton, is probably far better known as a popular interpreter of Christianity, the author of such works as *The Screwtape Letters* and *Mere Christianity.* He may be even better known as a writer of Christian fantasy in his trilogy of novels *(Out of the Silent Planet, Perelandra,* and *That Hideous Strength)* and in his Narnia series of children's stories, including *The Lion, the Witch, and the Wardrobe.* Tolkien created his own imaginative universe in *The Hobbit* and his "Ring" trilogy. Williams did not come from the same social class as the others and did not have the educational opportunities that had come to them. Instead of going to the university, he had to go to work. His work, however, was as an editor for the Oxford University Press. He became a member of their group when the O. U. P. was evacuated to Oxford during the war. His work ranged from a number of books written on assignment for extra income to complex poetry on themes from the Arthurian cycle, to studies of Dante. He is best known as a novelist who could write works in which the intervention of the supernatural could be not only credible but overwhelmingly convincing. These novels, such as *All Hallows Eve,* reflect a deep spirituality that can embrace both the mystical and the sacramental.

A friend of several of the Inklings though never a member of their group (she did not, after all, reside in Oxford) was *Dorothy L. Sayers,* whose Lord Peter Wimsey stories are some of the most popular crime fiction ever written. Although the last of these, *Busman's Honeymoon,* was written in 1937 — twenty years before her death in 1957 —they are regularly reissued in paperback even today and a number have been turned into plays seen on educational tv. The last years of Sayers' life were largely divided between duty as a popular theologian and defender of Christianity and work as a scholar and translator of Dante. The daughter of an Anglican priest, she was one of the first women to receive a degree from Oxford. Her field was medieval literature and her translation of the *Song of Roland* is classic. Her theological writings included essays such as are collected in *Creed or Chaos,* developed theses such as that argued in *The Mind of the Maker,* and many plays, including *The Zeal of Thy House* and *The Man Born to be King.*

The literary artist from a different tradition who has also made his Christian witness is the Russian novelist, *Aleksandr Solzhenitsyn,* who has written so convincingly about Soviet oppression. A plausible case could also be made for the inclusion of *Dag Hammarskjöld,* the Secretary General of the United Nations, whose work *Markings* posthumously revealed his mystical life, although there may be questions about his Christian orthodoxy. On the Roman Catholic side, surely consideration would have to be given to *Thomas Merton,* whose influence continues to grow, through his writings, long after his death.

If one looks for influential theologians to consider for future canonization, Anglicans would be as scarce as they have in earlier generations for this category. Two recent Archbishops of Canterbury would about take care of the matter. *William Temple,* trained as a philosopher in the English idealist tradition of the turn of the century, led Anglicans in becoming aware of the need for Christian social action and ecumenical commitment. His most important works in theology, as such, are *Mens Creatrix, Christus Veritas,* and *Nature, Man, and God.* Although Regius Professor of Divinity before he became Bishop of Durham in 1952, *Arthur Michael Ramsey* is probably better known for the force of his personhood (rather than personality) than for his contributions to the technical literature of theology. To be in his presence is obviously to be in the field of a great intellectual and spiritual force. He, too, was an active ecumenist, who worked closely with the Orthodox Church, visited Pope Paul VI, and sought union with the English Methodists.

The great names in Protestant theology during the twentieth century have been those of *Karl Barth* and *Paul Tillich.* Barth was a Swiss pastor when World War I revealed the shallowness of the liberal theology then being taught in German universities. That liberalism grew out of an optimism about human nature and the human mind derived from rapid progress in science and technology. The war and the suffering that followed convinced Barth that human intellect was corrupted with the rest of human nature by the power of sin and that the only dependable source of wisdom was the revelation of the Word of God. He considered philosophy to be of little assistance to the theological enterprise. The "Crisis" or "Neo-Orthodox" theology that he developed met with such a response that he came to say:

> *"As I look back upon my course, I seem to myself as one who, ascending the dark staircase of a church tower and trying to steady himself, reached for a banister, but got hold of the bell rope instead. To his great horror he had then to listen to what the great bell had sounded over him and not over him alone."*

Barth's opposition to Nazism forced him to leave the German universities in which he had been teaching and to return to his native Switzerland. Tillich was also a German and, to escape Nazism, came to the United States where he began an illustrious teaching career at Union Theological Seminary, New York. After retirement he went on to Harvard and then to the University of Chicago. Unlike Barth, he drew heavily on philosphy, especially phenomemology and existentialism. He was deeply influenced by psychological thought and socialism. His nearest approach to Barth's multi-volumed *Church Dogmatic* was his three-part *Systematic Theology.* His next most important work was *The Protestant Era,* although two volumes of his sermons, *The Shaking of the Foundations* and *The Courage to Be,* made his thought familiar to thousands of people to whom his more technical work would have been inaccessible. Barth and Tillich dominated Protestant theology for over a generation, and no one of similar influence has yet risen to their levels.

A major task for Roman Catholic theology in recent years has been to appropriate the theology of St. Thomas Acquinas for an age that has finally seen the implications of Immanuel Kant's assertion that the mind does not know things as they are in themselves but only in terms of the order imposed on sensation by the receiving intellect. The two most successful efforts at that task have been those of *Karl Rahner* and *Bernard Lonergan.* Rahner, a Jesuit, taught at Innsbruck before and after World War II, transferring to the faculty at Munich in 1964. As one of the editors of *Lexikon für Theologie und Kirche,* a ten-volumed encyclopedia of theology, he was able to have his insights widely spread. His thought is considered to be abstruse, but he was one of the theologians most influential at the Second Vatican Council.

Another Jesuit, Lonergan, has largely become known after the Council. A Canadian by birth, he began to exercise some international influence after he was invited to teach at the Gregorian University at Rome in 1953. Appropriately, he has been much concerned about theological method: how one goes about the theological task. His first important work, *Insight,* published in 1957, was a magisterial study of "the act of organizing intelligence that brings within a single perspective the insights of mathematicians, scientists, and men of common sense." Although he has written learnedly about the doctrines of the Trinity and Christ, his greatest impact has been in the area of "fundamental theology," which seeks to discover what makes theological thought a legitimate intellectual enterprise. Such work is important if one believes that intellectual re-evangelization must be carried forward in the Western culture. Since suffering from lung cancer in 1965, Lonergan has returned to Canada. Michael Novak identifies the contribution of Lonergan as giving Catholic theology both scientific and historical consciousness.

The list of candidates for future calendars who are theologians could be extended considerably: *Pierre Teilhard de Chardin* the Jesuit paleontologist, who used evolutionary concepts to develop a system of theology and spirituality; *Hans Küng,* who demonstrated the congruity of Roman Catholic understandings of justification by faith with Karl Barth's Reformed views on that subject, and who did so much to promote the theology of Vatican II; *Edward Schillebeeckx,* the Dominican who has written in such an illuminating way about sacraments, revelation, and the doctrine of Christ, and whose thought lies behind the Dutch Catechism; *Jean Daniélou,* who did as much as anyone else to show that historical-critical biblical study should not threaten Catholic orthodoxy; *Louis Bouyer,* whose writings did so much to awaken the Episcopal Church to the Liturgical Movement; and *Massey H. Shepherd,* the man most responsible for the Episcopal Church's 1979 Prayer Book. Theology is an area in which it would be possible to go on for some time praising famous men and women.

Other candidates for canonization in the future could be sought among those who have influenced the life of the church. Probably none has done so more than *Pope John XXIII,* who sought to let the fresh air of *aggiornamento* into the Roman Catholic Church by convening the Second Vatican Council. In recent time, the most influential Christian witness has often been made in the arena of social reform. There were, for instance, many Christian leaders who opposed Hitler — as well as all too many who capitulated to him and even cooperated with him. None of the resisters has captured Christian imagination in quite the way that *Dietrich Bonhoeffer* did. The commitment that led him to participate in the plot to overthrow Hitler, causing him to be imprisoned for two years and then hanged, speaks eloquently in his *Letters and Papers from Prison* and *The Cost of Discipleship.*

While Christian social witness is often thought to have been something invented in the civil rights movement of the '60s, it has always been a part of the work of Christ in the world and has always had its voices, however unheeded. Such witness has a marvelous example in *Dorothy Day,* who, along with Peter Maurin, founded the Catholic Worker Movement during the Great Depression. The principles they espoused included living in voluntary poverty while they fed the hungry, sheltered and homeless, opposed exploitation, advocated pacifism, and practiced a very strict and traditional Roman Catholic piety. Day, who had grown up in an atmosphere of affluence and social privilege had originally been drawn to the bohemian life of intellectuals and artists in New York in the twenties and her friends of that period represented an honor roll of American literature and the arts. She also became interested in social reform and went to work for the *Socialist Call.*

Her gratitude for the birth of a daughter in a common-law marriage, however, turned her to the church and to publishing the *Catholic Worker* while urging others to imitiate her in opening houses of hospitality for the poor. She carried on the struggle for almost fifty years before her death in 1981 and she kept up a consistent position of personal involvement rather than mass action. There were times when the work was popular and there were times when it was hated and attacked. She went to jail eight times, the last at the age of seventy-five when she picketed with Cesar Chavez and the United Farm Workers. Most of the Catholic radicals of the '60s and '70s could be considered as her disciples in some sense or other, although she would not have approved of all their tactics. Few have ever matched her commitment to the gospel precepts of feeding the hungry and caring for the homeless.

Undoubtedly the person who has best personified the Christian passion for social justice in recent years has been *Martin Luther King, Jr.* Beginning with the bus boycott in Montgomery, Alabama in the mid-50s and going on to his death from an assassin's bullet in Memphis in 1968, he set an example of non-violent efforts to change an oppressive social system that gave a new clarity to the meaning of Christian love. He knew how to hate the sin while loving the sinner and never gave up on the hope that God would change the hearts of bigots and fanatics. No one who heard it can ever forget the great vision he shared in his speech on the steps of the Lincoln Memorial as the climax of the March on Washington in 1963:

"I have a dream that one day on the red hills of Georgia the sons of former slaves and the sons of former slave owners will be able to sit down together at the table of brotherhood. I have a dream that one day the state of Mississippi, a state sweltering with the heat of oppression, will be transformed into an oasis of freedom and justice.

I have a dream . . . "

So great was the power of his vision that he was able to communicate it to millions who had never dared to dream before.

This list too could be extended indefinitely. I have a vivid memory of a "holy icon" that hung on our refrigerator for months, a photograph clipped from a newspaper that showed the war-resister, Father Daniel Berrigan, between the two F.B.I. agents who had arrested him at the Block Island home of William Stringfellow and Anthony Towne.

The smile on Berrigan's face was radiant, while the faces of the law officers were hard and grim. The obvious question that anyone who saw the picture had to ask was: "Who is captive here and who is free?"

There is, then, no obvious shortage of candidates for future calendars. Furthermore, this list has just touched on the most obvious candidates. An extraordinarily high percentage of the holy ones listed here have been Nobel prize winners, surely one of the most conspicuous forms of recognition a person can receive in our society.

Because of the very brightness of the public light in which these people have lived, however, it would be impossible for a reasonably well-informed person to read these names without thinking about reports that have been circulated about many of them that hardly seem consistent with the claim that they practiced heroic virtue. It is clear that many had feet of clay.

Prayer Book Studies IX, The Calendar, published in 1967, stated as one of the principles followed in the compilation of its list of persons to be commemorated that no one should be admitted until at least fifty years after his or her death. A good reason for that principle is that it takes that long to have perspective. The real value of the person is all that stands out after all that time (although, as Shakespeare's Mark Anthony reminded us, it can work out the other way). Certainly one gets the impression from history that many of the saints had horrible tempers. That was certainly true of St. Jerome and seems to have been true of James Lloyd Breck and Mother Cabrini.

The discovery that many of the saints did not practice heroic virtue in every aspect of their lives is not necessarily disappointing. One of the most widely-read spiritual writers of our time and perhaps also another candidate for future calendars is Henri Nouwen, who has written so eloquently about "the wounded healer." Maybe that is the only sort of healer there is. Certainly the Bible never attempts to whitewash its heroes. Abraham is depicted as passing his wife off as his sister several times so that he will not have to defend her honor against the efforts of powerful rulers to include her in their harems. Moses was not allowed to see the Promised Land because of his impatience and anger. David not only had Uriah the Hittite killed to cover up his adultery with Uriah's wife, but also proved himself to be incapable of disciplining his children. The personality of St. Paul comes across so vividly in his letters that many modern Christians do not admire him at all.

All down through church history the saints continue to be revealed as flawed persons. We think, for instance, of the orthodox Church Fathers who mobilized Egyptian monks to exercise mob control over the Ecumenical Councils of the church, leading one church historian to remark that the councils may have been infallible but they were not impeccable. To focus the question more sharply, we can notice that since the Reformation, Roman Catholics have canonized some who were involved in persecuting or discriminating against Anglicans and that in our calendar are Anglicans who have done the same thing to Roman Catholics. (This raises all sorts of questions. *Could God have inspired both the Reformation and the Counter-Reformation? Is God always on only one side? Can God call different individuals to do things that are apparently in conflict with one another? Must all the saints be "safe"? Do they all have to be "plaster"?*)

We do know that the most unexceptionable of persons all have their blind spots. In saying this I do not wish to excuse sin. But it is possible to become so absorbed in the paradox of grace that we appear to court what is ugly.

We also need credible, attainable models for imitation. In *The Cocktail Party,* T. S. Eliot wrote, "The best of a bad job is all any of us make of it — except of course, the saints." Yet what we have seen raises questions of whether it is such a package deal even for the saints. Apparently even the saints retain their basic character and disposition, which includes their flaws. There are many ways in which that could be phrased theologically. One is to say that we are justified by grace through faith rather than by our works and deserving. Another is to recall the four stages of the love of God listed by St. Bernard of Clairvaux:

1. The love of the self for the sake of the self.
2. The love of God for the sake of the self.
3. The love of God for the sake of God.
4. The love of the self for the sake of God.

This last, according to St. Bernard, is not attainable in this life. In other words, we will continue to sin as long as we are on this side of death. Yet within this sinful state God is able to transform us by the power of his love so that we will be ready for the final transformation.

When I was a young priest in the '50s, the ideal of sanctity was very popular. One frequently sung children's hymn was Lesbia Scott's "I sing a song of the saints of God." It was sung, as the directions call, "with vigor," and we always looked forward to the punchline: "For the saints of God are just folk like me, and I mean to be one too." No statement captured our priestly imaginations so much as, "In the final analysis, the only real tragedy is not being a saint." Sociologists can tell us how it is possible for an idea to meet a ready reception everywhere at certain times and to fall on dull ears at others. Whatever the explantion, most of the years between the '50s and now have been times when the ideal of being a saint sounded quaint, irrelevant, quixotic, or bizarre. Perhaps the time has come when this goal can be reconsidered out of the simple realization that *life is about God.* If St. Augustine was correct in believing that God has created us for himself and that our souls will be restless until they find rest in him, surely the most sensible thing we can do is to seek him with all our hearts. We may be a little more chastened and a little less naive as we do so. But we have the example of all the flawed persons who have gone before, whose lives have been wonderfully transformed because they were willing for God to accomplish his purposes through them. What T. S. Eliot said about the Crusades applies equally throughout most of church history and certainly in our time:

> *"Only faith could have done what was good of it,*
> *Whole faith of a few,*
> *Part faith of many.*
> *Not avarice, lechery, treachery,*
> *Envy, sloth, gluttony, jealousy, pride:*
> *It was not these that made the Crusades,*
> *But these that unmade them."*

> *"Remember the faith that took men from home*
> *At the call of a wandering preacher.*
> *Our age is an age of moderate virtue*
> *And of moderate vice*
> *When men will not lay down the Cross*
> *Because they will never assume it.*
> *Yet nothing is impossible, nothing,*
> *To men of faith and conviction.*
> *Let us therefore make perfect our will.*
> *O God, help us."*

— Chorus from "The Rock."

For Further Reading

Cunningham, Lawrence. *The Meaning of the Saints*. San Francisco, Harper & Row, 1980. A book written from a Roman Catholic perspective with an intention very similar to that of this book.

Brown, Peter. *The Cult of the Saints: Its Rise and Function in Latin Christianity*. Chicago, University of Chicago Press, 1981. A study by a distinguished modern scholar of the social purpose served by the development of the cult of saints, especially in forming a network of friendship and patronage between bishops after the conversion of Constantine made them a respected element in Roman society.

Lesser Feasts and Fasts. New York, Church Hymnal Corporation, 1980. The collects, epistles, and gospels for the minor fixed holy days in the 1979 Prayer Book together with short biographies of all the saints commemorated.

Veal, David L. *Saints Galore*. Cincinnati, Forward Movement, 1972. One page biographies of all the saints in *Prayer Book Studies IX*.

Harton, Sibyl. *Stars Appearing: Lives of Sixty-eight Saints of the Anglican Calendar*. London, Hodder and Stoughton, 1954. Several pages on each of the Black-Letter saints of the English Calendars of 1662 and 1928.

Cropper, Margaret. *Flame Touches Flame: Six Anglican Saints of the Seventeenth Century*. London, Longmans, Green & Co., 1949. Lives of George Herbert Nicholas Ferrar, Henry Vaughan, Jeremy Taylor, Margaret Godolphin, and Thomas Ken.

Walton, Isaac. *The Lives of Dr. John Donne, Sir Henry Wotton, Mr. Richard Hooker, Mr. George Herbert, and Dr. Robert Sanderson*. Various editions. A contemporary view of some of the same Caroline divines depicted in the foregoing modern volume.

Farmer, David Hugh. *The Oxford Dictionary of Saints*. Oxford, Oxford University Press, 1978. Short entries about almost 1,000 saints who appear in the English calendar, the Sarum rite, and the modern Roman Catholic calendar, or who otherwise have historical importance, especially in Great Britain.

Attwater, Donald. *The Penguin Dictionary of Saints*. Baltimore, Penguin Books, 1965. A handy paperback volume that covers about three-quarters as many saints as the book above. Its author is a distinguished English Roman Catholic scholar of the lives of saints and has published a number of books on the subject.

West, Morris L. *The Devil's Advocate*. N.Y. Wm. Morrow Co., 1959. An examination in novel form of the process of canonization.

McGinley, Phyllis, *Times Three, selected verse*. Garden City, Image Books 1975. Delightful light verse about saints and their humanity.

The Oxford Dictionary of the Christian Church and The Westminister Dictionary of Church History also have entries about many saints.